ARCHITECTURE & DESIGN LIBRARY

MOROCCAN STYLE

Alexandra Bonfante-Warren

FRIEDMAN/FAIRFAX
PUBLISHERS

A FRIEDMAN/FAIRFAX BOOK

Friedman/Fairfax Publishers
15 West 26th Street
New York, NY 10010
Telephone (212) 685-6610
Fax (212) 685-1307
www.metrobooks.com

Library of Congress Cataloging-in-Publication Data

Bonfante-Warren, Alexandra.
    Moroccan style / Alexandra Bonfante-Warren.
        p. cm. — (Architecture and design library)
    Includes index.
    ISBN 1-56799-956-5
    1. Interior decoration—Morocco. 2. Architecture—Morocco. I. Title. II. Architecture
and design library.
    NK2087.75 .B66 2000
    729′.0964—dc21   99-057931

Editor: Hallie Einhorn
Art Director: Jeff Batzli
Designer: Jennifer Markson
Photography Editor: Wendy Missan
Production: Richela Fabian and Camille Lee

Color separations by Colourscan Overseas Co. Pte. Ltd.
Printed in Hong Kong by Midas Printing Limited

1 3 5 7 9 10 8 6 4 2

Distributed by Sterling Publishing Co., Inc.
387 Park Avenue South
New York, NY 10016-8810
Orders and customer service: (800) 367-9692
Fax: (800) 542-7567
E-mail: custservice@sterlingpub.com
Website: www.sterlingpublishing.com

To Peter Warren and Ana Lillian Columna Warren,
remembering Beethoven's Seventh.

Contents

INTRODUCTION

Morocco has seduced the imagination of outsiders for centuries. From the whitewashed homes of the casbahs to the scented mazes of the souks, or market-places, to the glamour of Rick's Café Americain and *Casablanca*, this modern and ancient kingdom by the sea manages to be both familiar and exotic at the same time. Its style, preternaturally cosmopolitan and elegant, is admired in countries around the world and has been adapted in a wide variety of households. There is a trend to entertain guests more at home these days, so what better source to turn to for guidance than a culture in which hospitality is chief among virtues? The desire for comfort and serenity is easily fulfilled within a decorating idiom that is essentially spiritual in inspiration, but that also embraces pleasure in the manifold beauty of the tangible world.

Called El Maghrib al Aqsa—The Land Farthest West—by the conquering Arabs in the seventh century, Morocco and its history touch the Mediterranean Sea on the north; the vast, eternally shifting Sahara on the east and south; and the Atlantic depths on the west. This seemingly magical country, which is a monarchy, encompasses the drama of the great Atlas and Rif mountains, fertile lowland plains in the west, and dream ocean beaches, still virtually untouched by tourism, that gaze upon the boundless Atlantic. In busy cities, urbane crowds in veils, brightly hued djellabas (traditional ankle-length tunics worn by men and women), chic suits, and Paris fashions frequent sophisticated hotels and exquisite restaurants.

Layers of rich cultures have created this singular society, where only blocks from a fashionable street in Rabat (the royal capital), a teeming souk rings with the cries of merchants. And over it all every day, from the slender minarets that punctuate the skyline, the muezzins summon the faithful to prayer—sometimes over amplified public address systems.

Islam was brought to the area by Arabs traveling across North Africa thirteen hundred years ago. In the mosques, there is stillness,

OPPOSITE: *The heart of the traditional Moroccan home is the courtyard. A small fountain and lush greenery have transformed this one into a private oasis. Equally enticing is the room seen beyond, which beckons with its colorful, plump cushions and softening textiles.*

coolness, reflection, and worship. Complex configurations of blue tiles create not confusion, but a heavenly chorus of patterns, encouraging meditation and contemplation. Calligraphy, one of the great Muslim art forms, is most properly used in mosques when the name of Allah is written.

In the markets all is profusion. Stacks of elaborately etched trays, teapots, and rose water censers made of copper, brass, or tin are piled precariously beneath racks of traditional clothes in every shade and fabric. Fragrances of sandalwood, cinnamon, and the hot-pepper paste known as *harissa* mingle in a sensuous mélange. Distinct palettes merge in the jumble of shops, which are entirely open to the narrow streets. There are the dozens of gradations of powdered henna (which, in market squares, are presented in brown paper bags), the deep, saturated tints of skeins of wool in the dyers' districts, and the florals and stripes of contemporary fabrics. Wrapping through and over all, the ubiquitous sweet scent of mint tea suffuses the rhythms of the bazaar with graciousness, as youths bearing trays with glasses of the aromatic infusion or small cups of coffee thread their way through the throngs. The chaos of the souk is only superficial, however; shops are traditionally grouped by trade, then located relative to the nearest mosque according to a hierarchy of prestige dictated by the Koran.

Light years from the bustle of the souks is the comfort of Moroccan homes. Often, earth-toned walls provide handsome backdrops for banquettes upholstered in the geometric reds, blues, greens, and yellows of Rehamna carpets (which come from the plains near Marrakech)

R I G H T : *The snow-covered flanks of the High Atlas form a breathtaking backdrop for the tropical silhouettes of date palms and the outline of local architecture. The striking contrasts in the Moroccan landscape find their counterpart in the exquisite balance of traditional design elements.*

and for patterns that recur in numerous mediums. The Koran interprets the commandment against graven images as forbidding *any* literal depiction of *any* living part of creation. This prohibition has given rise to the bewitching, endlessly inventive designs seen in rugs, pottery, metalwork, woodwork, stucco, and *zillij*, the world-celebrated Moroccan tilework.

The patterns of textiles and ceramics are expressions that draw upon tradition but are not frozen in it. Like other features of Moroccan design, they are open to reinterpretation. For instance, a traditional pattern might be updated with contemporary colors. Furthermore,

ABOVE: *Architectural features in classic patterns and color combinations frame the view without competing with it. Notice how the smooth curves of the arches are juxtaposed against the angular lines of the battlement beyond.*

OPPOSITE: *Everything in this Moroccan gazebo welcomes friends, from the embrace of the structure to the convivial banquettes that invite relaxed conversation. Not only do the carved screens filter the seaside sunshine, but the arches they create add a lightheartedly formal accent that honors guests.*

elements of Moroccan design can be used sparingly in the home or incorporated lavishly—such is the flexibility of this unique style.

Moroccan style rings its changes throughout the country's great cities: Tangier, Fez, Rabat, Casablanca, Meknes (once the sultan's city), and Marrakech, where the brick-red dust of the nearby desert veils all. Then there are the sun-baked villages the colors of sand, which have not changed in a thousand years, except for the introduction of electricity and running water, and those conveniences not always, not everywhere. Farther east and south are the clusters of villages at the wadis, the oases where water, life itself, springs out of the desert. Beyond geography are the invisible, timeless trails of the nomads in their ceaseless transhumance. They are fewer and fewer, now, as the desert becomes increasingly arid and modern economies leave little room for the nomads' way of life.

Moroccan style is as profound and complex as its history and as multifarious as the many peoples whose cultures it has absorbed, from the native Berbers, to the Phoenicians and Romans, to the enduring influence of the Muslim Arabs, and the passing centuries of Portuguese, British, and French colonists. Yet, like many countries that have seen wave upon wave of invaders, Morocco is all the more deeply itself.

Perhaps Moroccan culture is above all the fabulous legacy of the near-legendary El Andalus, the medieval Islamic realm of southern Spain, which was finally defeated in 1492 by King Ferdinand and

LEFT: *Mud made magnificent in Marrakech. The mellow finish and deep color of the wall imbue the space with heartening warmth. Built-in cupboards lined with wood are accentuated by detailed carvings in a radiating pattern. The play of squares and rectangles continues in the fireplace, the mirror, and the bricks at the base of the wall.*

Queen Isabella. El Andalus was a place of scholars and artisans, of architecture and poetry, of developments in all aspects of living, including the physics and chemistry that made possible the colors of zillij, which would become the pride of Fez, and is currently enjoying a brilliant rebirth. (Morocco has a darker history, too; this was one of the countries of the infamous Barbary Coast, home and refuge of the pirates that plundered the Mediterranean for cargo and slaves.)

One of the most famous of the innumerable visitors to be seduced by Morocco's visual culture was the French master painter Henri Matisse, who was not only a great colorist, but a brilliant decorator of interiors—take a look at any number of his works. Dazzled by the light and shades of Morocco, Matisse drew upon the essence of these hues in his paintings of the country. The unmistakable reds are there, but even more so, the greens that appear in rugs, tiles, and glossy painted woods, from delicate tints of sea foam and sage to the saturated viridian of pure pigment.

Gourmets cite Moroccan cuisine as one of the world's greatest, for its inventiveness and ingenious combinations of flavors. The sweet and savory gastronomic alchemies blend the philosophies and ingredients of France, Spain, and North Africa into a unique synthesis. Likewise, this traditional and innovative culture has woven the best of Africa, Europe, and the Arab lands into an unmistakable manner of living, one that provides us with an ongoing invitation to refresh our senses and our spirit.

BELOW: *Moroccan decor's most characteristic colors, which recur in several mediums, reflect the rich hues of spices, such as cumin, paprika, and saffron. Here, containers of these seasonings rest on a classic pattern of local tiles.*

OPPOSITE: *Some nomadic Bedouin tribes still drive their sheep, goats, and camels along the timeless routes of their ancestors—with variations due to climatic and geopolitical changes. And many woolworkers still use organic dyes to achieve the striking hues that appear in carpets and other weavings from Morocco.*

CHAPTER ONE

EXOTIC EXTERIORS

In the casbahs, the oldest quarters of the oldest cities, thick-walled homes keep interiors cool during the searing Moroccan summers. The sturdy mud bricks that are still among the most commonly employed construction materials give characteristically rounded lines to buildings. For all its clean lines, Moroccan design leaves room for soft edges—it is never harsh.

The architecture expresses hospitality, one of the most powerful of basic human values. The humblest house will sport a decorated door that not only bespeaks the pride and personality of the residents, but gestures to outsiders. Traditionally, ornamentation—particularly color—has been used on exterior doors to prevent evil spirits from entering. Doors can take the shape of rectangles or arches. Some are wooden, while others display gleaming metalwork.

While hospitality plays a large role in Moroccan design, so does privacy, a fundamental yet delicate drive behind the Moroccan aesthetic. The most sumptuous contemporary villa outside Fez, a restored house in the old quarter of Meknes, and a modest home in a remote village all share outer walls that are virtually uninterrupted by architectural details, save for doors and windows. These walls may be painted in one of the many shades of the traditional earth-tone palette or in pale green, bright yellow, or light sea blue—hues also used in carpets and zillij. Or, they can simply manifest the natural color of the building material.

Behind these walls, the traditional Moroccan home has translated the ancient Roman atrium into an interior courtyard, around which the family's rooms open to refreshing light and air. A courtyard or garden often serves as an outdoor living room—so essential is it to Moroccan life that a house itself is sometimes referred to as a *riyadh*, which means an interior garden. It is here that Moroccan design has happily appropriated another Roman legacy, the column, for porches, loggias, and galleries. Here, too, spirituality plays a role, because gardens are considered to be earthly reflections of the Garden of Paradise. A garden may be no more than a few potted plants in a tiled courtyard or

OPPOSITE: *In a desert culture, where water is found is paradise enough. This swimming pool doubles as a reflecting pond in the lushly planted riyadh of the former home of Jacques Majorelle, a French painter who lived in Marrakech in the 1920s and 1930s.*

a wave of bougainvillea or heady-scented jasmine pouring down a wall; or it may be a compound, incorporating pavilions and other outbuildings, pools for swimming or meditation, and fountains to charm the ear and distract the mind from worldly cares.

Other architectural features that dot the Moroccan landscape are the characteristic domes, the crowning rows of ziggurat-shaped merlons, and the classic green roof tiles. All demonstrate the graceful functionality of Moroccan design. For instance, the curved shape of the roof tiles not only sheds rain, but also creates a pocket of insulation between the roof and ceiling, providing added protection against the heat; the characteristic domes do much the same, while supplying a feeling of amplitude.

Like other aspects of Moroccan style, the architecture reflects the culture's different influences and blends them into a striking form that is specifically Moroccan. Moreover, architectural devices are constantly being reinterpreted and molded to accommodate contemporary needs and preferences.

RIGHT: *Traditional Moroccan style: a timeless* ksar, *or fortress. The architecture demonstrates an elegance in its impeccable proportions and geometric details, from the vertical windows to the rounded, pointed arches to the angled bases of the various structures. The southern sunlight calls out the myriad earth tones.*

LEFT, TOP: *Sea blue and blossom pink adorn this wall of a restored farmhouse in Essaouira. The blue brings style to both the weathered wooden door and a deep window recess that is further enhanced by a simple pattern. For centuries, home owners throughout the Mediterranean have used blue to keep evil spirits at bay—a practice that is thought to have originated in ancient Egypt.*

LEFT, BOTTOM: *The doors of homes are often hand-painted in age-old patterns. This entrance reflects the rich use of color that permeates Moroccan design.*

RIGHT: *Today, skilled Moroccan artisans preserve and update a variety of time-honored crafts, including metalwork. A frankly modern pattern on these brass doors is balanced by a classic design in the oculus above and hospitably anchored by two gleaming traditional lanterns.*

OPPOSITE: *This classic fna, or central courtyard, uses bricks in a herringbone pattern for texture. The tiled threshold adds ceremony to the vaulted arch leading into the open-air space. A diminutive fountain and a series of pointed Moorish arches complete the picture.*

ABOVE: *This portal of the royal palace in Fez displays the geometric opulence of the contemporary tile master's art. On the underside of the arch, a tagguebbast, or sculpted plaster cornice, frames a raised starburst pattern, known as testir, in brass. To the right, calligraphic strokes transcribe the words of the Koran.*

A B O V E : *The dome is an architectural feature that is prevalent throughout the Arab world. Here, the rounded form provides contrast with the straight lines of earthy Moroccan bricks.*

RIGHT: *A traditional ziggurat pattern sculpts an expanse of pale azure sky above a wall the color of a desert ksar. In the foreground, bougainvillea, ceramics, and fruit manifest the hues that have inspired artisans and artists for centuries.*

OPPOSITE: *Nothing is more Moroccan than* pisé, *the adobelike sun-dried earth that is easily carved to create decorative surfaces. Because pisé is inexpensive to replace, it is often impossible to date many Moroccan buildings accurately. The wrought-iron grille in the window is contemporary.*

ABOVE: *Like other styles, Moroccan architecture has evolved with the times. While the columns, arches, lintels, and narrow bricks recall the influence of the Roman Empire, the overall design of this villa, located in the exclusive Palmerai area outside Marrakech, is essentially contemporary.*

ABOVE: *The traditional eight-pointed star shapes the infinity-edge pool of a Tangier villa. Imbuing the scene with a peaceful quality, the palette of immaculate white and deep blue emphasizes the sky and ocean.*

OPPOSITE: *Sinuous arches, a merlon-crowned wall, and soft corners of whitewashed adobe combine to create a Moroccan paradise in the middle of Los Angeles. The subtle geometric design skipping along the bottom of the walls is derived from zillij.*

CHAPTER TWO
INNER PARADISES

Home, like family, is the center of Moroccan life, an oasis of daily custom. Just as the door to the outside is painted to protect those within, so interior doors are decorated with ancient talismanic signs and symbols. In fact, the very word "talisman" is derived from Arabic.

However, not only doors are adorned. The Moroccans say that no wooden piece is complete until painted, but such surfaces can be carved, incised, gilded, stamped, or engraved with hot irons as well. The traditional technique of painting on wood is known as *zouak*.

While different types of wood are used in Moroccan homes, cedar is prevalent, since it requires no varnishing and boasts the ability to keep damaging insects at bay. A painted wooden shelf or coffer built into a wall is a classic feature, and the rich vocabulary of astral, geometric, and floral designs is often called upon to decorate wooden architectural elements, such as beams, lintels, shutters, and ceilings. The latter can be painted in strips like a Berber carpet or carved into magnificent *mukarnas*, vaulting bearing stalactite-like forms. Iron studs and brass nails often dot beams, while iron or brass strap hinges can grace doors. These elements create dramatic contrast against stucco or the sheen of *tadlekt*.

One of the textures that most immediately bespeaks Moroccan style is the glossy, leatherlike surface produced by tadlekt. This laboriously achieved waterproof wall and floor treatment was originally developed for the traditional steam bath, the *hammam*, but has since found its way into all parts of the home, appearing not only in bathrooms, but living rooms and bedrooms as well. The lustrous finish provides a flattering backdrop for furnishings and decorative accents.

Carved out of the thickness of interior walls, rounded niches are another hallmark of Moroccan design. These seamlessly integrated spots can host a collection of favorite books, a display of decorative objects, a dressing table, a home entertainment center, or even a sleeping alcove. In a similar fashion, a fireplace sheathed in the same plaster as the

OPPOSITE: *The visual appeal of this contemporary fireplace stems from a knowledgeable and ingenious combination of colors, patterns, shapes, and textures. From the desert palette and arched opening to the shine of the tiles and the gloss of the tadlekt finish, the hearth continuously exudes warmth, even without a glowing fire.*

surrounding wall seems to grow organically out of it. Decorated with tiles or painted wood, a hearth becomes a cozy (and practical) addition.

Perhaps the key to a Moroccan-style layout is a strict separation of public and private rooms. Ornate posts or a swath of fabric can be enough to make the distinction. The use of masonry columns or wooden pillars formalizes the movement between indoors and outdoors, whether in an arcade around a central courtyard or a second floor gallery. A balustrade on a balcony may be made of sinuous wrought iron or turned wood for a more rustic effect. Most traditional of all are the *moushrabiyas*. These screens are made of turned wooden knobs glued or nailed in a pattern into a frame, or of star or octagonal shapes cut out of a sheet of wood. In the strictest Islamic practice, these "harem screens" are placed at windows and above balconies so that the women of the household may look outside without being seen.

In contemporary designs, moushrabiyas make excellent shutters, gently filtering natural light into a room. Similarly, as room dividers, these versatile screens allow light to pass from one part of a room to the next. Wrought iron can add similar texture at windows, and painted, it makes an exotic statement. And arches provide yet another subtle means for sculpting interior space. When used without an accompanying door, a Moorish or horseshoe arch can create a smooth flow from one room to the next, while still lending definition. As with most other aspects of Moroccan design, interior architectural features can be adapted, altered, and reinterpreted to create a fresh look while maintaining a Moroccan essence.

LEFT: *A bedroom becomes sedately elegant with a few architectural flourishes: an arched niche, low zillij wainscoting with an antique air, and a molding of carved plaster arabesques. Well-worn carpets, traditional metalwork, and low wooden tables are fitting accoutrements for the surrounding architecture.*

OPPOSITE: *A row of classic eight-pointed stars becomes a subtle grace note on a wall bearing a warm, neutral stone color. Wooden screens mask shelves in a niche, and carved wooden furnishings bring charm to a conversation arrangement. Overhead, slender reeds between the beams contribute to the natural look of the space. This traditional type of ceiling is usually made of cedar or laurel that has been painted.*

ABOVE: *With its mirrored overmantel, a formal fireplace contributes a sense of grandeur to this comfortable and eclectic living room in a Tangier home. Simple terra-cotta flooring humbly defers to the elaborate painted ceiling, which presides majestically over all.*

OPPOSITE: *The view from the adjoining room, which boasts a more traditional Moroccan layout, reveals another aspect of the remarkable fireplace—its arch loosely echoes that of the passageway between the two spaces. The timeless colors of pomegranate and henna appear in a modern, custom-made carpet and the multitude of cushions. The touches of green in the light fixtures recall the patina of ancient bronze.*

ABOVE: *Sensual exoticism reigns in a Tangier villa. Antique yellow silk embroidery from Fez is flanked by open wooden doors, their panels painted in classic floral patterns that reveal the lush Persian influence. Handmade metal bolts contribute to the feeling of extravagance.*

RIGHT: *The Villa Taylor, built in the 1920s, is a nonpareil example of the Hispano-Moorish style. A showcase of Moroccan interior architecture, design, and craft, it has remained virtually unchanged since the days it welcomed such visitors as Winston Churchill. Elaborate zouak work and an intimate seating niche are just a couple of the characteristic elements that recall the past.*

OPPOSITE: *Light and shadows create drama in a hallway where one wall is an assemblage of moushrabiya panels. Not only do the screens keep the interior cool, but their carved openings and repeating patterns transform light into ornament.*

RIGHT: *A sliver of color transforms a window into a picture frame. When the winds from the Atlantic blow too cold onto this terrace of a Tangier villa, the residents just close the window and enjoy the tempered sunlight through the painted-white leading of the glass.*

LEFT: *Nothing detracts from the enduring grandeur of this palatial courtyard. The round glass table and arced chair legs discreetly gesture to the horseshoe arches, just as the horizontals of the chair backs add contrast and a hint of minimalism.*

OPPOSITE: *A color scheme of soft white and creamy lemon enhances the openness of this gallery. The rhythmic sequence of the arches and an antique lantern bearing stained-glass accents heighten the appeal of the space.*

LEFT: *The triumph of taste in this modern bathroom is an elegant sum of shrewdly simple parts: the severe geometry of the fixtures (a semicircle and a rectangle), such humble materials as brick and terracotta, and the absence of superfluities, such as a shower curtain and window shades.*

ABOVE, LEFT: *This handsome shade of green provides a perfect foil for any object occupying the built-in display niche. The slight texture provided by the glazing on the tadlekt surface accentuates the patterns in the pierced-metal bedside table and the ornate bedstead.*

ABOVE, RIGHT: *The luxury in this Moroccan home is understated, thanks in part to the green tadlekt, finished with an additional glaze—a successful example of gilding the lily. A slender window illuminates a cozy alcove with built-in seating, perfect for intimate conversation, meditation, or dreaming.*

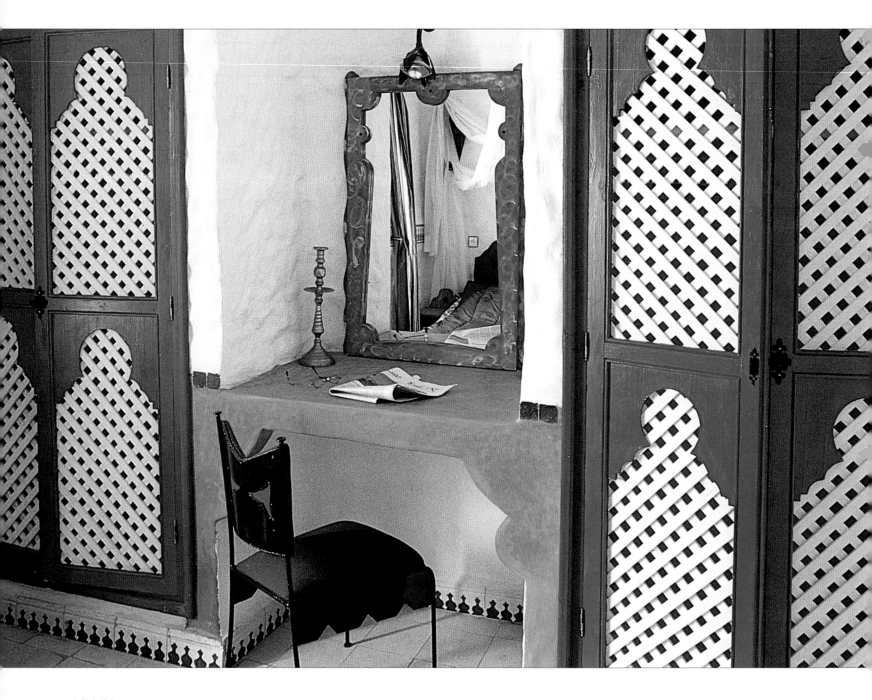

ABOVE: *This dressing room is enhanced by those most elemental of Moroccan colors, cobalt blue and cloud white, which recall the medieval pottery of El Andalus. A dressing table has been ingeniously built into a niche between the closets, with a clever paint treatment creating the illusion of legs. The closet doors are spiced up with crisp latticework, giving the space an airy quality.*

RIGHT: *Seen through graceful Moorish arches, the shimmering blue sea becomes part of the decor in this tranquil bedroom. The interior also features a centuries-old beamed ceiling and a relaxed mix of patterns.*

CHAPTER THREE
GRACIOUS DECORS

Moroccan decor is a sublime balancing act, a harmony of simplicity and elegant profusion. Thanks to its equilibrium, this instantly recognizable aesthetic abounds with interpretive flexibility, allowing decorating fantasies to take form while remaining true to the idiom's essential authenticity. The secret lies in identifying the basic elements and modifying them to fulfill individual needs, tastes, and preferences.

Color is the heart of the matter. Morocco's white is the dazzling white of clouds over the Atlas Mountains; its reds are the classic hues of Berber textiles. Walls, whether in the living areas or bedrooms, often boast shades of sand and spices. The rich reds of paprika, the sun tint of saffron couscous, and the muted earth colors of turmeric and cumin all imbue a space with a Moroccan flavor, especially when combined with the textures of tadlekt or lacquer.

While the European tradition tends to use furniture and color to define a room's function quite rigidly, Moroccan style is far more fluid. One of the primary furnishings is the couch, a banquette that lines the wall. Here is the heart of hospitality, a welcoming statement of comfort, a place where family and friends meet for conversation while enjoying the traditional mint tea. A low carved wooden base supporting a vast brass tray or a tabletop inlaid with zillij or mother-of-pearl adds a formal touch to the intimacy of a tête-à-tête or the liveliness of a banquet.

For an exotic touch, a seating platform lavishly layered with thick pile carpets and huge pillows harks back to the nomads' tents. A great room can be the scene of a feast for all senses with allover color and striking accents.

A few pieces of stained glass, a shock of exotic blossoms in a classic ceramic pot, and a tone is set. So unique is Moroccan style that just a few expressive items are enough to endow an area with its unmistakable imprint. Not surprisingly, some of the most decorative objects revolve around the pleasure of sharing good food and drink: a brass bread dish; pottery or antique copper *tajines*, used for serving the subtly fragrant Moroccan stew of the same name; an antique wooden or silver sugar hammer; a tea service, with a silver pot and intricately worked tea box. While these accessories are highly decorative in and of themselves, they can also enhance a decor by taking on new roles.

OPPOSITE: *A snug sofa curves alluringly, welcoming whispered confidences and the relaxed fun of informal dining. Low lamps enhance the intimacy, as do the horizontal stripes, which break up the room's height. The warm shine of metal and the stucco window treatment (the blue color of which offers a preview of the sky beyond) stamp the decor as Moroccan.*

For instance, a tin container that once held tea can make a stunning home for a small bouquet of flowers.

The glint of metal contributes to the enchanting allure of many Moroccan-style rooms. Whether it appears in a procession of tin lanterns, a brass jewel casket, or a petite side table, incised and pierced in timeless patterns, handcrafted metal enlivens its surroundings with a touch of pizzazz. The luster of brass becomes especially beautiful when playing off the warmth of earth tones.

In the bedroom, Moroccan style can conjure an air of magic and romance. Picture a bed draped with a tentlike canopy of diaphanous materials. Such accents as a lantern or metal-framed mirror can enhance the play of light and heighten the ambience. A Moroccan-style bedroom can also exude tremendous warmth. A low-slung bed covered in flat weaves, carved wooden furnishings, and tadlekt walls in rich reds, oranges, or yellows combine to create an atmosphere of comfort.

Whether they're outfitting a living room, dining room, or bedroom, Moroccan furnishings and accessories provide visual delight. And above all, they imbue the areas they adorn with one-of-a-kind Moroccan grace.

LEFT: *A delicate, carefully balanced use of rich color is what gives this dining spot its appeal. Mimicking a sunrise, the combination of blue, yellow, and red beckons residents and guests to relax and enjoy the view.*

ABOVE: *The hot colors of paprika and saffron, as well as the encircling couches that line the wall, distill the essence of Moroccan style. The low table and traditional tea service bring home design back to hospitable basics.*

LEFT: *Beautifully carved and inlaid wooden furnishings imbue this room with understated elegance. The color of the seat cushions echoes the earthy hue on the walls for a unified effect.*

ABOVE: *Guests may refresh themselves with a sprinkle of rose water from these traditional vessels, which also make beautiful decorative accents. The distinctive scent, mingling with the aromas of tea and mint, will heighten a Moroccan ambience.*

OPPOSITE: *The Roman influence prevails in this airy dining room, especially in the architecture of the display case, the busts on the side table, and the handsome X-frame chairs with their prominent brass rivets. Yet all it takes is an antique brass lantern to inject a specifically Moroccan flair.*

ABOVE: *This is color with assurance and no holds barred—Moroccan modern in all its uninhibited splendor. The tassels on the chairs nod to those on the hoods of traditional djellabas, while a modest ceramic jar takes on the high tone of its surroundings. Lush greenery and flowers evoke the image of an oasis.*

BELOW: *It only takes a few well-chosen details to imbue a space with a Moroccan flavor. In this accommodating kitchen, good things come in threes. A triad of antique lanterns points to the vaulted ceiling, while three decorative tajines line up on the counter. A more workaday version of the latter sits on the range.*

ABOVE: *Moroccan style is more than just a look: it is, for those who care to make it so, a way of life. Here, fragrance, shade, and texture meet in a glass of mint tea, a metal chalice of raisins, a graceful teapot, and an etched metal tray. While the traditional vessels are currently performing their intended service, these beautiful pieces can easily act as decorative accessories on an end table or coffee table.*

ABOVE: *Simple comfort is the seductive force behind this Moroccan-style living room. With clean lines and pure white upholstery, banquette-like couches beckon residents and guests to relax. A round wooden tabletop echoes the soft curve of the hearth while serving as a counterpoint to the L-shaped configuration of the seating. It is this careful juxtaposition of rectangular and rounded features that gives the space a keen sense of balance.*

ABOVE: *An incredible painted simulation of zillij transports the occupants of this North American bedroom to the sensual land of Morocco. The vivid pattern sets off a quasi-rustic chest of drawers, while the eye-catching geometry of a studded box carries the focus upward to the reflective play of the mirror.*

RIGHT: *Outfitted in the colors of sun-baked Moroccan earth, this bedroom entices. While just a few pieces furnish the space, the room does not seem empty, thanks to the warmth of its hues. The headboard recalls the ubiquitous arches, while the embellishment at its center immediately draws the eye. Note the dazzling zillij tabletop that appears in the adjoining sitting area.*

OPPOSITE: *A lavish use of Moroccan elements allows occupants to sleep in the lap of luxury. From the gleaming metalwork of the mirror and doorways to the romantic canopy bed and sumptuous upholstered furnishings, the space exudes a majestic tone. Two rugs rest on sea blue wall-to-wall carpeting to define the different areas of the room.*

ABOVE: *A clean-lined modern chaise longue is right at home amid classic Moroccan-style elements. The combination just goes to show how accepting and flexible Moroccan design is.*

ABOVE: *With its luscious yellow walls and rich persimmon orange carpeting, this seductive bedroom envelops its occupants in warmth. A green antique ceramic pot and a sky blue wooden table are the telling details in this understated ensemble.*

ABOVE: *The strength of this room lies in its clear statement of values: simplicity, beauty, and comfort. The warm palettes of timeless Berber textile patterns stand out solidly against whitewashed walls.*

ABOVE: *Mud brick walls, a carved wooden headboard, and a colorful bedspread work together to create a rich medley of textures. Fresh flowers contribute natural texture while drawing out the pinkish hue in the bed covering.*

OPPOSITE: *Tadlekt, originally devised to provide waterproof surfaces in the hammam, returns to its original function in a modern bathroom. The highly detailed wooden mirror frames, a colorful table with legs carved to form the outlines of Moorish arches, and a charming tin accessory give the space a furnished look. Any one of these elements would be enough to lend a room a Moroccan air.*

CHAPTER FOUR

WOVEN WONDERS

One of the most striking areas in a Moroccan souk is the dyers' quarter, with its breathtaking array of saturated hues destined to be woven or knotted into beautiful works of textile art. At one time, among the Berbers, particular woven designs were associated with specific clans or tribes, but these patterns were not rigidly fixed, since a woman who married into a clan would bring her own family's or clan's designs into the mix. Plus, ample room has always been left for individual creativity.

Weavers have been practicing their craft in Morocco for some thirty-five hundred years. The Phoenicians, the most famous dyers of the ancient Mediterranean world, are credited with having taught the Berbers their secrets. Even though synthetic dyes have been used since the beginning of the twentieth century, plant and mineral pigments are still called upon frequently. There is poetry in their employment: madder for the characteristic dark reds and orangish reds; pomegranates and dried figs for blacks; tea and henna for reds and browns; and saffron, almond leaves, and various flowers for yellows. Indigo, still employed for clothing fabric in the Sahara, has been replaced by chemical dyes. For the most part, the fibers are sheep's wool, sometimes with goat or camel hair added. Cotton is used for white details, and small amounts of silk for brightness.

Berber and Arab designs are almost exclusively geometric. Berber rugs, which are fashioned by women, tend to be relatively loosely woven elongated rectangles made up of horizontal strips of design. They were originally used as blankets. One of the pre-Islamic beliefs still held among the Berbers is that of the *baraka*, or supernatural power, of crafted objects, among other things; symbols intended to deflect the evil eye are interspersed with tribal signs in woven textiles. The so-called city carpets—generally made by men using the knotted-pile method—are thick and quite rigid. Their symmetrical compositions are usually square or less markedly rectangular, while their patterns are variations on traditional Turkish or Persian designs.

The manifold patterns allow Moroccan textiles to be combined with zillij designs for an opulent effect that is underscored by the

OPPOSITE: *Primary colors take on mystical connotations when they appear in shades reminiscent of the Moroccan landscape. Neatness accounts for the visual appeal of this bedroom: the soft weaves fall in such a way as to preserve the rectangular lines of the bed and bedside table while tempering the hard edges of the tin mirror.*

suppleness of the fabrics. The opposite works, too, with dense textile compositions providing accents in predominantly white rooms or amid natural, neutral shades.

In traditional surroundings, rugs and huge pillows invite family and guests to while away the hours in deep conversation and easy silences. Designed to be portable, Moroccan textiles allow you to create a lavish environment wherever the fancy takes you—and to whatever degree delights you. These versatile decorative elements can be called upon to cover banquettes, enhance beds, or adorn and insulate walls. The energy of reds, orangish reds, and yellows creates exciting drama against a white wall, whose chastity stands in contrast to the sensual layerings of fabric. Multicolored patterns make ideal backdrops for carved wood and shaped metal.

In contemporary homes, textiles can be used to inject a little fantasy into a space. For instance, gauzy fabric can be draped around a banquette in a tentlike fashion, with a more sober vintage rug anchoring the space below. Whether a room is adorned with just one magnificent rug or layered with textile upon textile, these soft elements will contribute much richness to the decor.

ABOVE: *A kilim—which simply means "woven" in Arabic—covers a sofa that exudes a sensuous feel, thanks to a drift of cushions in an array of hues and textures. Not in the classic white, but in a wisp of rose, a canopy awaits the moment to create a romantic tenting à deux.*

OPPOSITE: *Designed to avoid the cold look inherent in the traditional bathroom of European descent, this welcoming space is adorned with textiles and wood furnishings. In the midst of its present company, an antique tub looks more like modernist sculpture. Notice how the colors of the geometric-patterned square on the wall serve as a link to the nontraditional floral designs of the painted cupboard.*

LEFT: *What should be excess is stunning elegance—such is the alchemy of high Moroccan style in a room with perfect proportions. A skillful blending of colors and patterns gives the room a seamless look. A Rabat carpet, identifiable by its double borders, holds pride of place in the center of the mix.*

ABOVE: *In this elongated space, an array of carpets provides a foil for the wood ceiling. Although the carpets are different from one another, they are tied together by the one color that they all share—red.*

LEFT: *All is volume and texture here, from the high tented ceiling and velvety panels to the sheen and deep colors of heavy silk. Fabric covers every surface, resulting in an enveloping effect that is utterly sensual.*

ABOVE, LEFT: *A generous showing of textiles encourages relaxation in this alluring living area. Three different but compatible fabric designs create a delightful mélange, which is heightened by the texture of the woolly carpet and the graphic impact of tile and inlaid wood.*

ABOVE, RIGHT: *An unexpected use of a tentlike canopy can infuse a space with a nomadic sense of adventure. Here, a red canopy of fine wool not only shelters a wooden chair, but also provides contrast with the rough texture and ocher hue of the walls.*

OPPOSITE: *The dark hues of the textiles and furnishings in this living room make a dramatic statement against the yellow walls. Lengths of plum-colored fabric swathed around a city window and draped over a side table recall the many shades of desert indigo and set the tone for the woven tribal designs on the floor and furniture.*

RIGHT: *This supple wall hanging boasts a riot of shades and patterns. Instead of being mounted flat against the wall, the wool fabric is allowed to fall in columnar, almost architectural, folds, which echo the lines of the candlesticks.*

LEFT: *Stimulating hues in an unadorned dining room put the focus where it belongs: on the guests and the closeness of a shared meal. A sumptuous, yellow wool shawl with a reddish-orange border rests atop a monochromatic tablecloth, creating ceremony without stuffiness.*

ABOVE: *In this stately dining area, a plain tablecloth is overlayed with hand-embroidered silk from Fez. A ceramic bowl of fresh flowers provides a fitting centerpiece, echoing the magenta blooms of the textile.*

LEFT: *Part of the appeal of Moroccan design lies in its adaptability. While this bedroom relies heavily upon textiles for comfort and embellishment, the colors are anything but traditional. In a similar vein, the decorative bands below the ceiling and atop the "wainscoting" reprise timeless zillij patterns, though no actual tiles are used.*

ABOVE: *Building upon the basic homes of nomadic tribes, this bedroom tent is a lighthearted compendium of Moroccan motifs.*
A blue and white color scheme predominates, faux-Roman columns bear alabaster vases, and the painting on the left recalls
Eugène Delacroix's desert horsemen.

LEFT: *Wall hangings of undyed wool keep this room cozy during winter. Casually draped fabrics, including a Saharan batik, cohabit with an antique tajine for a relaxed interpretation of classic Moroccan style.*

ABOVE: *This rooftop hideaway boasts an enticing divan, neatly draped and pillowed in unusual fabrics for receiving guests—or for sleeping amid palm-swept breezes on sultry nights. A lithe wooden chair, paired with a handy painted table, provides an ideal spot for reading or simply basking in solitude.*

CHAPTER FIVE

TIMELESS TILES

The ceramic arts, among the world's most ancient, occupy a special place in the realm of Moroccan crafts. Scholars believe that the first pottery arrived in North Africa some eight thousand years ago. During the course of the twentieth century, however, imported ceramics and plastic housewares acquired greater status among Moroccans than domestically made pottery. This trend caused many skilled ceramists to turn their efforts toward tile making. (Fortunately, a recent rise in the demand for "art" pottery has largely revived the ancient craft.)

The Arabs brought the Persian practice of tiled ornamentation to Morocco, where it met the Roman mosaic tradition of creating pictures from tiny tesserae, or tiles. The Persians used only blue and white in their tilework, a characteristic that initially came from China. Blue and yellow ceramics are reminders of the Portuguese occupation of certain Moroccan ports, while solid green recalls the much earlier Roman occupation. The many vivid colors increasingly made possible over the centuries by improved technologies are entirely a Berber characteristic; of all the Islamic countries, Morocco alone boasts this rainbow palette.

Paradoxically, the golden age of Moroccan ceramics did not take place in Morocco but in El Andalus, where polychrome pottery was produced. When the Moors were driven out of Spain by King Ferdinand and Queen Isabella, these people took their wondrous cut-tile art, zillij, to Morocco, where it was preserved within guilds often made up of men and boys from a single family. Because Islam prohibits the literal depiction of living things, the mesmerizing designs of zillij are purely geometric.

Over the centuries, zillij nearly died out, and understandably so. It is a craft that requires an almost unimaginable body of knowledge: some 360 shapes exist, so the mathematical permutations are virtually infinite—even without bringing color into the mix. There is a vast number of traditional patterns that the *zlayiyyah*, or tile master, knows by heart. Not surprisingly, an apprenticeship may take six or seven years. Like the patchwork quilts of which North Americans are inevitably reminded, many of the designs have names—one of the most expressive translates as "Makes You Crazy."

OPPOSITE: *Handmade brass lanterns cast an enchanting glow in this splendid fna. A tile pattern in the ancient Roman style leads to an intricate, supremely harmonious design centered on a classic eight-pointed star.*

Zillij is enormously time-consuming and expensive: it can take more than four thousand worker-hours to lay four hundred square feet (37sq m) of an especially elaborate design. Although long used almost only in palaces and mosques—where, according to Berber tradition, the patterns aid meditation, even draw the worshiper into a trance— zillij has entered the realm of residential interior design.

Today, these mosaics are sometimes treated like prized carpets and used sparingly. Other tastes call for a lavish use of this precious tilework over large surfaces in courtyards, bathrooms, kitchens, and even living rooms and bedrooms. Whether in the verdant expanse of a garden, or the artful touch of a stair riser, the timeless beauty of Moroccan tilework adds a little bit of paradise to any home.

BELOW: *A contemporary wall of zillij graces this open-air lounging area. The tile design in the foreground reminds us that the Dutch artist Maurits Cornelis Escher, the master of mysterious perspective, was greatly influenced by zillij.*

OPPOSITE: *Restoration meets revisionism: the traditional green roof tiles typical of Moroccan constructions are here almost aqua. As a result, they serve as a link to the pool, which has been designed with a twist on the contemporary infinity edge. Notice how the continuous use of tiles from the sitting area into the pool echoes the flowing motion of water.*

OPPOSITE: *The tile flooring's muted earth tones contribute to the natural look of this peaceful courtyard, which is graced by a venerable tree and potted plants. A tiled bench provides the perfect spot for reading the stirring poems of Al-Khansa, a seventh-century writer considered to be one of the most important female poets in Arabic literature. Lanterns sprinkled here and there add ambience.*

ABOVE: *Built in the customary manner around a courtyard, this residence has a swimming pool in lieu of a central fountain. When not in use, the pool's stillness merges with the serenity that arises from the repetition of the tile patterns.*

LEFT: *These columns display various traditional applications of zillij. A narrow band at the bottom sets the column apart from the floor; above it rises the main pattern, surmounted by the braid and then the crestings. The icing on the cake is the intricate sheath at the top.*

RIGHT: *Once merely practical, a fountain trough in an alcove has remained an appealing architectural convention. Here, East meets West in the tile patterns of the floor and surround and in the play of arched forms (one of which appears in the tilework). Rows of tiles on the risers create a dynamic graphic effect.*

ABOVE: *A contemporary kitchen is spiced up with a dash of Moroccan style, thanks to colorful mosaics on the*
cupboard doors. Additional tiles form geometric patterns on the countertop and backsplash.

ABOVE, LEFT: *Zillij is quintessentially versatile. A sixteen-pointed star pattern, in classic blue, yellow, and brown, lines a window ledge and finds a worthy companion in a blue tiled outdoor table. Traditional Islamic tile designs reflect the religious notion of "no beginning and no end."*

ABOVE, RIGHT: *A cheerful application of tilework on a backgammon table and combination mirror/hat rack demonstrates a whimsical adaptation of the ancient Roman mosaics unearthed in Morocco. Tesserae, the small colored tiles used by the Romans, serve as edging.*

ABOVE, LEFT: *Turmeric-colored bands of tilework, emphasized by the hues of the upholstery and cushions, create a reference to Moroccan carpets. A mirror resting on the floor extends the tile pattern, doubling the beauty.*

ABOVE, RIGHT: *It has been noted that zillij can be an aid to meditation. This particular application, formulated by an American designer working in Morocco, certainly lends itself to firelit musings.*

ABOVE: *Like other elements of Moroccan design, the use of zillij continues to evolve. In this sitting area, the art form has been called upon for a large part of the floor, making a grand gesture to those who enter. Contemporary versions of age-old patterns have been painted on the chairs.*

ABOVE: *A conventional European bathroom takes on Moroccan style with an impeccable mix of tiles—the uneven, handmade finish of which reflects light as gloss rather than shine. The crowning pattern on the wall is the stepped-pyramid design.*

RIGHT: *The classical Roman influence is evident in the rigorous verticals and horizontals of the tilework, although the color contrast of turmeric and reddish brown, edged elegantly in green and black, is pure Moroccan. To enhance the effect, a tadlekt finish gives the gloss of travertine.*

Copyright © 1986, Neugebauer Press, Salzburg–Munich–London–Boston
Published by PICTURE BOOK STUDIO, an imprint of Neugebauer Press.
Distributed in USA by Alphabet Press, Natick, MA.
Distributed in Canada by Vanwell Publishing, St. Catharines, Ont.
Distributed in UK by Ragged Bears, Andover.
Distributed in Australia by Hodder & Stoughton Australia Pty, Ltd.
All rights reserved.
Printed in Austria.

LIBRARY OF CONGRESS CATALOGING IN PUBLICATION DATA

Wilde, Oscar, 1854-1900.
The Canterville ghost.

Summary: A celebrated and feared English ghost is outraged when the
new American owners of his haunting place refuse to take him seriously
and actually fight back against him.
[1. Ghost–Fiction. 2.England–Fiction]
I. Zwerger, Lisbeth, ill. II. Title.
PZ7.W64583Can   1986   [Fic]   86-8179
ISBN 0-88708-027-8

Ask your bookseller for these other PICTURE BOOK STUDIO classics
illustrated by Lisbeth Zwerger:

THE GIFT OF THE MAGI by O. Henry
THE NUTCRACKER by E.T.A. Hoffmann
THE NIGHTINGALE by Hans Christian Andersen
LITTLE RED CAP by The Brothers Grimm
THE STRANGE CHILD by E.T.A. Hoffmann
HANSEL AND GRETEL by The Brothers Grimm
THE SEVEN RAVENS by The Brothers Grimm
THE SWINEHERD by Hans Christian Andersen
THUMBELINE by Hans Christian Andersen
THE LEGEND OF ROSEPETAL by Clemens Brentano
THE DELIVERERS OF THEIR COUNTRY by Edith Nesbit
THE SELFISH GIANT by Oscar Wilde